How to Hold a Garage Sale

How to Hold a Garage Sale

James Michael ULLMAN

A Benjamin Company Book   Charles Scribner's Sons New York

1 3 5 7 9 11 13 15 17 19 B/C 20 18 16 14 12 10 8 6 4 2
1 3 5 7 9 11 13 15 17 19 B/P 20 18 16 14 12 10 8 6 4 2

Printed in the United States of America
Library of Congress Catalog Card Number 72–11300
SBN 684–13283–4 (cloth)
SBN 684–13287–7 (paper)

Illustrations by Karl Stuecklen

DEDICATION

To those untold millions who, since time began and in all languages, have ventured into the thriving market in household goods by posting that magic "SALE" sign at their residence.

CONTENTS

1   WHAT THIS BOOK IS ALL ABOUT
Factors Behind the Trend ● Who Holds House Sales? ● What Is a "Successful" Sale? ● How Much Can You Make? ● Think of Yourself as a Store   11

2   THE TWO MOST IMPORTANT THINGS YOU MUST KNOW
Who Will Be At Your Sale? ● What They All Have in Common ● The "First Day" Phenomenon ● Pace of a Typical Sale ● What This Means to You   17

3   THE FIRST STEP: MARKET RESEARCH
Check the Laws ● Visit Other Sales ● Is It Junk or "Junque"? ● Elderly Sellers Should Learn Values   23

4   ORGANIZING YOUR SALE
Where Will You Hold It? ● What Time of Year Will You Hold It? ● What Day or Days Will You Hold It? ● What Time of Day Should You Hold It? ● What Will You Try to Sell?   30

5   YOU'LL NEED HELP—BUT HOW MUCH?
The Joint Sale: Pros and Cons ● Types of Joint Sales ● Should You Take Items on Consignment? ● Rules for Consignment Sellers ● How Much Commission Should You Charge?   37

6   HOW TO ADVERTISE YOUR SALE
Use Free Advertising • The Importance of "Word of Mouth" Advertising • Advertise in Local Newspapers • What to Say in Your Ads • Outdoor Advertising • Signs Attract People • Help Buyers Find You   45

7   ALL ABOUT PRICING
Why Everything Should Be Priced • How Much Should It Cost? • You Can't Ask Store Prices in a Garage • You're in a "Wholesale Market" • You Can't Win Them All • To Bargain or Not to Bargain? • Keep an Open Mind   53

8   LAST-MINUTE PREPARATIONS
What Kind of Tags? • Clean Up Your Merchandise • Point-of-Sale Signs • Be Ready to Make Change • Know What You'll Do with Your Money • Have a Credit Policy • Set Up Your "Command Headquarters" • Help Them Carry It Away   62

9   DON'T MAKE IT LOOK TOO MUCH LIKE A STORE
Displaying Your Merchandise • Special Outdoor Problems • Sales Promotion Devices   70

10   HERE COME THE "EARLY BIRDS"
What These People Really Want • Should You—or Shouldn't You? • Why We Don't Let Them in   75

11   SECURITY AT YOUR SALE
Guarding Against Shoplifters • Don't Leave Your "Store" Unattended • How to Handle Shoplifters • Other Security Problems   80

12   THE SALE BEGINS—AND YOU'RE ON YOUR OWN
You and Your Customers • They Won't All Buy • Honesty Really Is the Best Policy • Learn as You Go Along • When the Sale Is Over   86

APPENDIX A   HOUSE AND GARAGE SALE CHECKLIST   93
APPENDIX B   KEEPING RECORDS FOR JOINT AND CONSIGNMENT SALES   95
APPENDIX C   TYPICAL NEWSPAPER ADS   99

How to Hold a Garage Sale

What This Book Is All About 1

This book is about any sale in which you use your residence, or any part of it, as your "store."

The best-known sale of this type is the "garage sale," but you don't need a garage to hold one. For purposes of this book, the phrase can be used interchangeably with "house sale," "estate sale," "rummage sale," "basement sale," "breezeway sale," "patio sale," "back-porch sale," "barn sale," "yard sale," "sidewalk sale," "moving sale," "residue sale," "tag sale," or any other name you think best describes your venture.

Generally the items offered at these sales are used household goods. These can range from appliances, tools, toys, clothing, furniture, furnishings, books, sporting goods, and bric-a-brac to valuable antiques and works of art.

Some sellers also offer new merchandise obtained from businesses where they work or at auctions, bankruptcy sales and similar outlets. These people will also find this book helpful, although primarily it is aimed at sellers of used household merchandise.

Although a few sellers are full- or part-time dealers moving some of their merchandise through their own homes, most garage- and house-sale sellers are amateurs and many are holding their sale for the first time. It is to help these "first-timers" especially that this book has been written.

FACTORS BEHIND THE TREND

If you're thinking of holding a garage sale or one of its many variations, you have plenty of company.

These sales are proliferating all over the United States, especially in small towns, suburbs, and residential city neighborhoods. They are more commonplace in those localities because houses and apartments are usually larger, it's easier for customers to find parking places, and security is less of a problem than in many high-density city neighborhoods.

Behind the growing popularity of house and garage sales is the

12

fact that more and more people are deciding it makes good money sense to sell no-longer-wanted household items rather than throw or give them away.

At the same time, other people are looking for ways to make their money go further. At the house or garage sale they can buy things they may need for a fraction of their price new. The days of spending to "keep up with the Joneses" seem to be fading, while there's growing agreement that the smart thing to do with money is to put as much of it to work in savings accounts and other investments as possible.

Another force giving a big push to the rise of the garage sale is the so-called "nostalgia kick." More and more people want artifacts and mementos of days gone by. Usually the cheapest place to find them is at the house or garage sale, where what's trash to the seller may be a treasure to the buyer.

WHO HOLDS HOUSE SALES?

Most house sales are held by:

- People who are moving but don't want to take many of their possessions with them.
- People who just want to get rid of some stuff cluttering their house or apartment. Some women hold sales once or twice a year just to clean out their attics, closets, or basements.
- Small community groups trying to raise funds. The "garage sale" can be to the Cub Scout troop what the rummage sale is to the church.

- People combining the "housekeeping" motive with the desire to make a profit, however small, on the sale of some items they may have picked up at other garage sales, auctions, flea markets, etc.
- People hoping to make a profit on practically everything they are offering at the sale. In effect, no matter what their main source of income, these people are also at least semiprofessional "junque" dealers ("junque" being a catch-all phrase covering almost anything "collectible" that is not old enough to be a true antique).

WHAT IS A "SUCCESSFUL" SALE?

Given these many reasons for holding a sale, it's obvious that what is a "successful" sale for one person would not be a success to someone else.

For instance, if you're moving, almost any price for an item would be better than being stuck with it unsold when the sale is over. But if you're trying to sell at a profit, your price will be dictated by what you paid for the item.

If you're not obsessed with turning a profit on most of the things you sell, it will be much easier to have a "successful" sale than otherwise.

In this connection, bear in mind that the "regulars" who haunt house and garage sales include some of the world's most dollar-wise shoppers. Many have been studying their markets for decades, and they know the current wholesale price ranges of practically everything you will be showing. Turning a consistent profit when selling to them is not easy.

HOW MUCH CAN YOU MAKE?

The big question everyone thinking of holding a house or garage sale for the first time asks is: How much will I get out of it?

Again, it all depends. The variables include what you have to sell, where you live, the weather on the day or days of your sale, and how wisely (or unwisely) you plan and handle your sale and price your merchandise.

In doing research on this book, my wife and I have met sellers who claimed to have sold up to a thousand dollars' worth and more in sales running from a few days to a week. These people had owned fine furniture, appliances in good condition, and perhaps a few objects of art and were disposing of practically everything in their houses.

We've also interviewed housewives who have put out a few worn articles of clothing, some battered toys, and nondescript household bric-a-brac and cleared just twenty or thirty dollars over a similar span. Still, a housewife might regard this as satisfactory if it resulted in exchanging junk in her closet for some extra spending money.

Generally speaking, if you live in an area where the "garage sale" has developed a good following, have a wide selection of things to sell, and price your merchandise realistically, you will probably average from fifty to one hundred dollars per day over the course of a sale running from two to three days. If you are moving and disposing of practically everything in your house, you should expect to do better than that.

THINK OF YOURSELF AS A STORE

As this book will show, the house or garage sale is in many ways a minuscule version of any retail discount-store operation.

For the most part, it is self-service. Usually, people pick out their merchandise, bring it to a checkout counter, and pay for it there, but occasionally a customer asks the "clerk" for assistance.

Beyond this, to do the most effective job, sellers at house and garage sales must address themselves to such typical retailing problems as market research, advertising, sales promotion, pricing, merchandise display, credit, and store security.

The Two Most Important Things You Must Know **2**

Whatever your reasons for holding a house sale, you can vastly increase your chances of success by following a few general principles. These principles are based on the experiences of many successful sellers and stem from:

- An understanding of why people go to house sales.
- An understanding of what happens at a typical sale.

If you have never held a house or garage sale before, these are the two most important things you will learn from this book.

WHO WILL BE AT YOUR SALE?

In one sense, the people who come to your sale will be prompted by a wide range of motives. It's impossible to categorize all of them, but among the major groups are:

- Your friends, relatives, and neighbors. Because they know you, many will be among your best customers.
- People looking for a specific household item for which they have an immediate use.
- People looking for any household item for which they think they may have a use sooner or later.
- Junque addicts. These are people who haunt house sales, flea markets, auctions, etc., because they are addicted to buying "junque."
- Collectors. Many, but not all, collectors are also junque addicts. What distinguishes the collector is his (or her) specialization. Collectors know in exhausting detail nearly all there is to know about their subject, including rock-bottom prices.
- Dealers. They probably won't identify themselves, but at least a few of your customers may be junque or antique dealers. Usually they'll come at the beginning, hoping to find an unrecog-

18

nized treasure, or at the end, hoping to sweep up whatever's left for practically nothing, or both.

* People who are bored and go to these sales primarily to have something to do. In time they may become junque addicts. But meanwhile, they'll do much more looking than buying.

WHAT THEY ALL HAVE IN COMMON

No matter how diverse these peoples' motives may be in one sense, in another they'll come to your sale for the same reason. They're all looking for a bargain. This is the common element linking all buyers at house or garage sales. Otherwise they wouldn't be poking around in your garage, they'd be shopping in a store.

In fact many garage-sale "regulars" will buy anything if they think the price is right, even if they have no immediate use for the item. Either they plan to put it to use "some day" or hope to resell the item at a higher price, perhaps at their own garage sale.

An appreciation of this is crucial if you are to make the most of your sale. It means you must provide as many bargains as you can and make it known that these bargains exist.

THE "FIRST DAY" PHENOMENON

The other thing you must know if your sale is to be as successful as possible is that *no matter how long you run it, the first few hours will probably be the most crucial.* You'll probably have more potential customers and sell more merchandise during this period than during the remainder of the sale.

There are exceptions to this rule, especially in rural areas where population is sparse and buyers must travel long distances. Your opening-hour traffic may also be held down by bad weather, inadequate advertising and promotion, a bad starting time, or an unusually large number of competing sales starting on the same day. And sometimes, a number of buyers seeking last-minute bargains will show up during the final hours of a sale.

But certainly most sellers in relatively populous areas where the garage sale has attracted a following of buyers who attend them more or less regularly can anticipate that their heaviest traffic will be at the outset.

Why is this? It's because, all other things being equal, the people who attend these sales regularly want to go to sales beginning that day, and they want to get there as early as they can. They believe that if a sale has already been running for a while, the biggest bargains have been snatched up. They hope to see what you have before anyone else does.

PACE OF A TYPICAL SALE

Let's say you're planning a two-day sale to run Friday and Saturday. Typically, your sale would be paced something like this:

FRIDAY—You've announced the opening time for 9:30 a.m.,

but the first buyers arrive early. From 8:30 to 8:45 or so on, traffic will be very heavy until about 11 a.m. and will continue fairly heavy until noon, when mothers must be home to prepare meals for their children. During the afternoon the pace will be less hectic but steady.

SATURDAY—At the opening, only one or two buyers will trickle in. Nevertheless there will be a slow, steady stream of people turning up as the day proceeds. A few customers will be people who first visited your sale Friday and are returning for "another look around." Question your customers and you'll learn that a surprising proportion of your second-day visitors are casual passersby attracted by signs you have posted on the street.

WHAT THIS MEANS TO YOU

The most important thing this means to you is that you must allow plenty of time in which to get ready.

This can't be overemphasized. *The most common mistake made by people holding a sale for the first time is that of not being ready when the sale begins.* Some items are not tagged and many sellers don't even have their merchandise out where potential buyers can see it. And as more and more visitors tramp through the sales area, pawing through merchandise and asking questions, these sellers fall further and further behind.

There are many good reasons for being ready when the sale begins. The most important of them are that if you are not ready:

21

- Many would-be buyers will leave before they have had a chance to see everything you want to sell.
- You'll lose other sales because you didn't have merchandise tagged or you quoted too high a price "off the top of your head."
- You also risk selling things for far less than they're worth if forced to quote prices "off the top of your head."

To repeat: In planning your sale, allow plenty of time for preparations. If you're not ready when the sale begins you won't be able to take full advantage of what are potentially your most productive selling hours.

The First Step: Market Research 3

If you've never held a house or garage sale before, begin by doing some market research.

Any good businessman spends time and money studying his market before opening a new store or introducing a new product, and so should you. This book can give you general rules to follow in holding a sale, but those rules must be modified by the conditions and practices where you live.

23

CHECK THE LAWS

Talk to people who have held sales and phone or visit your city hall if necessary to learn if any local laws will affect you.

In most cases, none will apply. But some communities have laws regulating the number and duration of garage or house sales which you can hold during the year. There may also be restrictions on the placement of signs advertising your sale.

In addition, certain items may be subject to laws and regulations. Especially, check local, state, and federal laws before trying to sell firearms, ammunition, or explosives. Other local ordinances may cover the sale of such things as bedding, certain types of clothing, and food. Some communities may require that you apply for a permit to hold a house or garage sale.

There are even a few communities where garage and house sales are banned altogether. Usually this happens when a few greedy householders abuse the privilege and hold sales week after week, turning their homes or garages into virtual stores. In some cases antique and junk dealers have tried to avoid license fees or other restrictions by marketing their wares through their homes or through homes they rent from others.

In any event, where laws banning these sales exist they result from pressure brought on your lawmakers by local merchants who don't like the competition.

VISIT OTHER SALES

Much of your market research should involve visiting other sales in your area for the purpose of:

1. *Seeing How Others Do It.* The more sales you attend as a customer, the better you'll be able to plan your own sale. Seeing other peoples' sales will give you ideas on such things as where in your home or apartment to hold your sale, how and where to place signs, and how to display your merchandise.

Even more important, it will give you the customers' perspective. You'll soon learn what you personally like about the way some sales are held and dislike about others. What you like, other people will probably like too.

2. *Checking Local Price Levels.* Many items offered at other house and garage sales in your town or neighborhood will be similar or even identical to items you plan to sell. See what your neighbors are asking for those items. More important, try to learn if people are actually buying at those prices.

The world of the garage sale is a pricing jungle. Some sellers want too much for what they're selling and others don't want enough. Some have firm price levels but others are willing to lower prices substantially for the first person who shows interest or makes a serious offer.

A word of warning: when shopping around, you may have the experience of pointing to an unmarked item, asking its price, and being asked in return: "How much will you give me for it?"

This evasion of your question is an unfair selling tactic. The person selling the item should have some idea of its value and is obligated to quote a price, even if willing to reduce it later during a bargaining session. If any seller tries to pull this stunt on you, mumble something polite and get out of there before you find you've bought something you don't want for a lot more than it's worth.

3. *Questioning Holders of Successful Sales.* The best local advice on how to hold your own sale will come from people who have held successful sales of their own. When doing your market research, look especially for sales that seem to be going well. Then strike up a conversation with the person running the sale.

Tell the seller you plan to hold a sale of your own, and see how much you can learn. Usually, if approached cordially, people will be glad to share their knowledge with you.

But *don't* pester people with questions when they're busy selling merchandise to other customers. If necessary, come back at the end of the sale, when your sources will have more time in which to talk. A good question to ask at that time is what they'd do differently if they had it to do over again.

IS IT JUNK OR "JUNQUE"?

If you plan to sell household items and bric-a-brac scrounged from your attic, closets, and basement, you should also visit a few antique stores and shows, resale shops, flea markets, and perhaps an antique auction or two. This is to learn if some of the household "junk" you plan to sell is actually "junque"—i.e., items sought by antique buffs and collectors for one reason or another.

Many people don't realize that today an item doesn't have to be a century old (which is the formal qualification for an "antique") to be wanted.

If it's what dealers call "collectible," there may be a big demand for it. There are collectors for an infinitely wide variety of things mass-marketed and widely distributed during the lifetimes of still-living Americans.

These "collectibles" range from Shirley Temple mugs, Buck Rogers pistols, Tootsietoys, straight-edged razors, milk bottles and Coca-Cola thermometers to old fruit jars, pulp magazines, comic books, dolls, cast-iron toys, advertising memorabilia, glassware, ceramic whiskey bottles and country-store fixtures.

What's more, the list of "collectibles" is expanding rapidly. There is an economic reason for this. Prices of many items traditionally sought by antique buffs have been bid up so high that only the most affluent can now afford them. This induces people with collecting instincts but more modest budgets to seek new and less expensive things to collect. And of course the "nostalgia kick" is driving more and more people to start buying mementos of yesteryear.

So many items are being bought up by collectors today that no one book could even begin to catalog them all, although several have tried. If you go to any of the larger antique shows, you'll see some of thousands of books published on one category of collecting or another.

Generally speaking, the items most in demand by collectors are those no longer being produced which have a touch of "Americana" about them.

ELDERLY SELLERS SHOULD LEARN VALUES

When you hold a house or garage sale, you become part of a thriving "wholesale market" for collectibles and junque. These sales are avidly patronized by small junque and antique dealers as well as by collectors.

Many of these people are hoping they can buy for practically nothing collectibles whose true value is unknown to the seller.

The people most likely to sell junque for far less than it is worth are senior citizens. Perhaps that's because it is not easy to realize that items once so commonplace as to be valueless in their own lifetime now have antiquarian value. Older couples preparing to move and elderly widows or widowers breaking up their households often let items go for a fraction of their wholesale value. Older people especially should research the junque market to be sure they are not victimized by knowledgeable buyers.

Of course your visits to antique shops might disclose that your household junk is indeed what you first thought it to be—junk. You may also find that even though some of your junk is "junque," it is low-priced junque. On the other hand, you may be pleasantly surprised at the high price tags on some things you first thought were worthless.

If you have some time before your sale, one way to protect yourself is to begin studying periodicals that carry a heavy budget of buy-and-sell advertising for junque.

28

Some leading publications in this field are:
The Antique Trader, P.O. Box 1050, Dubuque, Iowa 52001.
Collector's News, Box 156, Grundy Center, Iowa 50638.
Collector's Weekly, Kermit, Texas 79745.
Hobbies, 1006 S. Michigan, Chicago, Ill. 60605.

Organizing Your Sale

4

Before you get very far along with the plans for your sale, you'll have to make some basic decisions. In part they'll be determined by your market research, but also they may be dictated by circumstances beyond your control.

WHERE WILL YOU HOLD IT?

All things being equal, it's a lot easier to hold a sale if you live in a house rather than an apartment. But wherever you hold it, the "sale" area should be clearly set off from all other areas.

Ideally, there should be natural barriers between the sale and nonsale areas. The garage sale is the perfect example of this. Everything for sale is displayed in the garage (and perhaps the outside approaches to the garage.) All other parts of your property are clearly "off limits" to buyers.

The "yard sale" is another good example. All merchandise is out in the yard. Customers have nowhere else to go.

If you live in a house and plan to hold your sale in your garage or yard, you have no problem. But if you're going to hold it in your apartment or in a basement, porch, patio, or what have you, you may have to create artificial barriers between your sale and non-sale areas. Otherwise, customers may invade nonsale areas and rummage through your personal belongings on the theory that everything is for sale.

These artificial barriers will depend on the layout. You may want to close doors, move furniture around, or hang curtains. Often, all that's needed is to post signs marking the limits of the sale area.

Try to locate the sale area as close as possible to the door through which people will be entering or leaving. This makes it easier to keep your customers in the sale area. It also helps protect your floor.

If it rains or snows on the day of your sale, assume the worst. Some people will be thoughtful and remove wet or muddy galoshes before stepping inside, but others will not. By putting your sale area close to exterior doors, you may save a lot of wear on the interior of your house or apartment.

WHAT TIME OF YEAR WILL YOU HOLD IT?

My wife and I once held a two-day sale in January. We live in Illinois. On the eve of our sale a mass of Arctic air moved in from the north, dropping the temperature to twenty below zero. All of fourteen people showed up on the first day and nobody came on the second day.

The moral of this story is that if you can avoid holding a sale on a weekend when the temperature could get as low as twenty below zero, by all means do so.

Extremely hot weather won't stop many people from coming to your sale, but very cold weather will. So will snow, ice, and heavy rain. If at all possible, avoid holding your sale at times of the year when the probability of any of these things happening is greatest. In most parts of the United States, the best times for a sale are between mid-spring and mid-fall.

If you live in a central or northern climate, you can do especially well with a sale in early spring, provided you are lucky enough to schedule it when the weather is good. In the weeks after a long, snowbound winter, the housewives who patronize these sales flock to them with more than usual intensity.

WHAT DAY OR DAYS WILL YOU HOLD IT?

The days when you hold your sale may be limited by your job, family responsibilities, or some other factor. But if you have a choice, here are some things to consider:

- *The longer your sale lasts, the less you'll probably sell on each sale day.* If you have a lot of time and want to keep your sale going until everything is sold, then by all means schedule a sale running for a week or more. But otherwise, you'll probably be better off limiting your sale to one, two, or three days, depending on how much time you can or are willing to devote to the venture.
- *Sale days near or on the weekend are better than days early in the week.* Thursdays, Fridays, and Saturdays are the traditional "garage sale" days in many areas, and many sellers with busy weekday work schedules hold their sales on Saturdays and Sundays.

Because of this, most garage-sale buffs plan on doing their "junking" on or near the weekend. Also, paydays usually fall at the end of the week, putting more cash in the hands of your potential buyers. If you plan to sell a lot of tools or other items used mostly by men, your sale should extend at least into Saturday. Many men like to patronize these sales but are unable to do so except on weekends because of their work schedules.

- *Publication dates of the newspapers carrying your ads could be a factor in selecting your sale days.* The best starting day would be the day after the publication date. This would give all readers, even those who get their paper late in the day, time to plan to be at your sale when it begins the following morning.

WHAT TIME OF DAY SHOULD YOU HOLD IT?

Your sale hours may also be determined by circumstances beyond your control.

If you have a choice, the best time would be from 9:00 or 9:30 a.m. until whatever hour you wish to finish. Starting times are more important than finishing times.

That's because no matter what starting time you select, some people will probably show up early. If you complete most of your preparations the night before and set a 9 a.m. starting time, you'll be ready as soon as most of your customers are.

But if you set a starting time for noon or later, planning to complete your last-minute preparations in the morning, people will show up all morning anyhow. They'll interrupt you long before you're ready for them.

Of course you can refuse to allow anyone in until your midday starting time. But bear in mind that many garage-sale "regulars" plan their "junking" trips with lists of every sale beginning that day, no matter what the announced starting time. If you turn all of these early arrivals away—and they include potentially your best customers—some won't bother to come back.

WHAT WILL YOU TRY TO SELL?

This question is not as simple as it seems. In deciding what to sell at your house or garage sale, keep an open mind. The type and variety of things you have to sell will be a big factor in determining whether your sale will be a success. Generally speaking:

34

- *The more things you offer for sale, the more you are likely to sell.* A large display of merchandise induces customers to stick around longer, looking everything over carefully to be sure they don't miss anything. The longer they linger, the more likely they'll find something to buy.

- *No matter how useless an item may seem to you, someone may want it.* Anything might go. The rotting lumber under your porch, the rusted bicycle wheel in your garage, the no-longer-working radio or phonograph gathering dust in the closet—haul all those things out for your sale and put a price on them, no matter how minimal.

- *Have a lot of items in the low-price range.* Your main concern in holding a sale may be to dispose of some expensive antiques, appliances, or furniture, but even this will be easier if you have plenty of low-priced merchandise for sale, too. The more low-priced items you have, the more things people will buy. Sales generate more sales. The "buying spirit" is infectious. People seeing other people walking out with armloads of merchandise will get in the spirit and begin buying too.

Another reason for having a lot of low-priced items is that many housewives who go to these sales operate on a limited budget. They have only so much to spend. If most of your merchandise is in a medium or high-priced bracket, you price many of these people out of your market. With a good selection of lower-priced items, you're giving all your customers as many chances to buy as possible.

- *Have items to interest children.* Even if you have no children of your own, offer a few simple, durable old toys or dolls that you've picked up for a song at rummage sales or other garage sales while doing your market research. While children play with these, their parents will have much more time in which to look around at the things you really want to sell.

You'll Need Help—
But How Much?

5

The more things you can find to sell, the more work you'll have to do to make the sale a success. You'll want all the help you can get, both from the point of view of making the sale go smoothly and for reasons of security. (For more details on security, see Chapter 11.)

If you're part of a family living together, enlist as many family members as you can for the project. If you're living alone, consider asking a friend, neighbor, or relative to give you a hand "minding the store" while the sale is going on, at least during the first few hours.

THE JOINT SALE: PROS AND CONS

One way to get help for your sale would be to let others in on it.

There are many pros and cons about the joint sale, in which two or more sellers pool their efforts.

The joint sale has become popular in many communities. It spreads the work load and gives buyers a much bigger selection of merchandise. It is especially good for neighboring housewives or families who share many social activities anyhow. Often the communal garage sale can be made a semisocial event that combines business with pleasure.

On the other hand, before organizing or agreeing to take part in a joint sale, be sure you know you can get along with the other member or members of the selling group.

Many decisions will have to be made and many problems will arise. If members of the selling group are not compatible, there'll be squabbling and bad feelings when the partners disagree. The resulting hostility will effect the efficiency with which the sale is run and cause you to lose both money and friends.

The main disadvantage of the joint sale is that you are no longer in control. Others may be making decisions for you. If this would disturb you, by all means avoid the joint sale.

TYPES OF JOINT SALES

If you decide on a joint sale and can get people to agree to go in on one with you, your next decision is what type of joint sale it will be.

Usually, in a joint sale all merchandise is hauled to the house or apartment of one member of the group and sold there. If you do this, your group must set up a record-keeping system ensuring that all purchases are accurately credited to the right sellers.

Many groups do this by coding all price tags to identify each seller. Each item is listed as it is sold. If the tags are removable, they might also be pulled from items and pasted to a ''Sold'' sheet, for tabulation later.

Whatever the mechanics of your system, accounts are settled at the end of each day or when the sale is over.

There are also joint sales in which each member of the group has his or her own selling space in the selling area. In effect, this is a small-scale flea market, with each seller responsible for his own merchandise.

This eliminates a lot of cumbersome record-keeping. But it also means all members of the selling group must be present nearly all the time. In addition, it may confuse and discourage buyers. People who go to house and garage sales are accustomed to wandering around, picking up items, and then paying for the whole lot as they leave.

Whatever system you use, in any joint sale all members of the group must fully understand the system before the sale begins. Responsibilities during the sale should also be clearly designated.

If the selling group is large—joint sales involving up to ten or twelve families or even an entire block have been held in some neighborhoods—it might also be a good idea to elect a sale chairman. That person would have final authority to settle disputes and make key decisions.

In a variation of the joint sale where sellers have adjoining houses or apartments, each group member displays and sells on his own property. In this case the sale's "joint" aspects are mainly in agreeing on sale dates and pooling funds and efforts in a cooperative advertising program.

SHOULD YOU TAKE ITEMS ON CONSIGNMENT?

You can assemble a greater variety of items to sell by taking some things on consignment from your friends, relatives, or neighbors. These items are displayed with yours. If you sell any, you get a commission.

Consignment sales can be a mixed blessing. In addition to giving you a greater variety of items, they get more people interested in your sale. Rest assured, people who bring items they want you to sell for them will help promote your sale through word-of-mouth. And of course, the commissions you earn will add to your profits.

On the other hand, you may not want to feel responsible for other people's merchandise or to be bothered with the record-keeping that may be involved. Consignment selling also poses potential hazards that could result in misunderstandings or disputes, ruining what had been beautiful friendships. There's also the chance that some consignors would abuse the privilege, loading you with too many items or items you'd rather not handle.

RULES FOR CONSIGNMENT SELLERS

If you do decide to take things on consignment:

- *Have it clearly understood that you won't be responsible if items are damaged or stolen.* If dealing with people who are not close friends of yours, or if the items are especially valuable, it might be wise to have this understanding formalized in writing.
- *Set up a system to credit consignment sales accurately.* As with joint sales, you could code price tags to identify each seller and then list each item as it is sold; or if you are using removable tags, they could be pulled from the items when sold and pasted to a sheet for tabulation later.

Still another system would be to assign each consignor a code letter. Then require them to tag and number their own items and to provide you with a list of them. Using this system, when a consigned item is sold, all you have to do is make a notation or checkmark on the consignor's list. (See Appendix B for examples of all three methods.)

If you make payments to a consignor during the sale, keep a record of that, too. In the confusion of a sale, it's easier to forget these things than you may think.

- *Don't be afraid to exercise control over what your consig-*

41

nors want you to sell. Hopefully, the problem won't arise. But it's possible one or more consignors will put prices on their items that you know are far too high. If they do, for your own protection, insist that they lower their prices to a more realistic level. People who come to your sale will assume everything on display is yours. If they see even a single item priced far more than they know it's worth, they'll categorize you as a price gouger.

It's also possible that, for reasons of taste or personal preference, you'd want to control the type of items offered by your consignors. Since it is your sale, insist on any criteria you wish. Likewise, don't hesitate to call a halt if any consignor brings more items than you want to handle.

HOW MUCH COMMISSION SHOULD YOU CHARGE?

The phrase "ten-per-center" has been popularized in novels, movies, and television dramas involving theatrical or literary agents. Probably that's why many people holding house or garage sales charge only a ten per cent commission when they take consignments.

In my opinion, under normal circumstances that's not nearly enough.

By "normal circumstances," I mean a sale in which the consignor does nothing but list and tag merchandise and then bring it to the site of the sale; and in which the person holding the sale must pay for all advertising, make and set out signs and other promotional materials, and then supervise the sale as it proceeds.

The difference between a literary or theatrical agent and someone holding a garage sale is that literary and theatrical agents sell talent, while people holding garage sales sell merchandise, usually second-hand.

Entertainers and authors have invested years of time and effort in developing their talents, perfecting their acts, and writing their books. They are entitled to most of the fruits of their labors, and the agents who handle them contribute only their ability as negotiators and salesmen. But the only things your consignors contribute are used household goods that may even be inferior to what you are selling.

At the other end of the scale, the owners of resale and consignment shops usually demand one-third or even one-half of the selling price of what you bring them.

However, the people who run these shops must rent a store, get a license, take out insurance, and meet all other expenses of running a year-around business, including salaries. They also devote their year-around time to the operation and have developed personal contacts with antique dealers, collectors, and other big buyers who visit their shops regularly.

The one-third to one-half cut is justified by the contributions which professional shopowners make, but may be too high for people running house or garage sales.

Generally speaking, a commission of twenty to twenty-five per cent for handling consignment items at a house or garage sale would be reasonable and fair.

This could be modified by circumstances. If your consignors give you meaningful help in financing or running your sale, you

should reduce the rate or eliminate it. Taking things on consignment could also be a way to repay a friend or neighbor for helping
you "mind the store" while the sale is going on.

Of course a big factor will be your relationship with the consignor. If he or she is an old or dear friend, you may not want to
charge a commission under any circumstances.

How to Advertise Your Sale

6

In gathering material for this book, my wife and I talked to a lot of people who have held house or garage sales on the "spur of the moment" and done very well.

For instance, if the weather's nice and they find they have no other plans for a weekend, some families quickly assemble and tag some merchandise, put up a sign or two announcing a sale and sit back to await buyers.

If you enjoy holding these sales, this can be a profitable and stimulating activity for one family alone or several working together. Certainly from an economic standpoint it beats a weekend in which you spend money for entertainment rather than making money while entertaining yourself.

But to be at all successful, a sale held on this extemporaneous basis must be on or near a high-traffic street or highway. And whatever the sale's results, it would have been more successful if you had promoted your sale properly.

The more people who hear about your sale, the more potential buyers you'll attract. The "spur of the moment" sale is fine if you understand its limitations. But for the maximum financial return from a house or garage sale, you must take the time to plan and carry out a well-rounded advertising campaign.

USE FREE ADVERTISING

Many stores and other business places have bulletin boards on which you can post a free advance notice of your sale. In many parts of the country, these bulletin boards are especially common in supermarkets.

In posting your notices, don't restrict yourself to the supermarkets in your immediate neighborhood. Spend an hour or two putting notices on any bulletin board within a reasonable driving range of the site of your sale.

In addition, merchants who know you may allow you to post signs in their windows. And if you or a member of your family work where there is a company bulletin board, see about posting a notice there. Similarly, it may be possible for you to post notices on bulletin boards of church, civic, or fraternal organizations to which you belong.

THE IMPORTANCE OF "WORD-OF-MOUTH" ADVERTISING

The most effective free advertising of all is "word-of-mouth" advertising spread by people who know you.

Tell your friends, relatives, neighbors, and co-workers about your sale. They'll be potential customers themselves and will tell their friends, relatives, and neighbors—especially if they know someone who might be in the market for some of the more expensive items you want to sell.

ADVERTISE IN LOCAL NEWSPAPERS

Generally speaking, it's a big mistake to try to cut your selling expenses by eliminating newspaper advertising. The only times this would pay would be when you had very little to sell or lived in a community so small and isolated that nearly all of your potential buyers would learn about your sale in some other way.

Newspaper advertising is essential because this is how most hard-core garage- and house-sale buffs learn about sales. They follow the classified columns in their daily, weekly, and community papers very closely. Many even use the advertisements to map out their garage- and house-sale "routes" for the day.

47

On the other hand, when planning your newspaper advertising campaign, don't go overboard and spend more than necessary.

If many papers serve your community, concentrate on the one (or ones) that will do you the most good. You can get some good advice on this from other sellers when you do your market research. As a rule, the most effective papers will be the ones with the greatest number of "Garage Sale" ads.

You'll also want to be sure to place your advertising *when* it will do you the most good. Learn the advertising deadlines of your newspapers. If you're advertising in a daily paper, your ad (or ads) should not appear until a day or two before the sale. If you're advertising in a weekly, advertise the week the sale is to start.

There are at least two good reasons why it doesn't pay to advertise too far in advance. First, most garage-sale customers are interested only in sales they can go to "right now." Second, early advertising may bring you a more than usual number of "early birds" who will interrupt your last-minute preparations by trying to see your merchandise several days ahead of time.

WHAT TO SAY IN YOUR ADS

In writing your ads, it's not necessary to get fancy or "cute." Just stick to the facts.

Don't waste money going into unnecessary details. Your ads shouldn't be sparse, but a few well-chosen words or phrases can be enough to suggest a diversity of merchandise. For instance, such phrases as "much miscellaneous," "loads of junque," etc., will be enough to show you have a lot of things to sell. And instead of just announcing a "Garage Sale," call it a "Mammoth Garage Sale," "Giant Garage Sale," or what have you.

If you're trying to sell some especially rare or valuable items, consider mentioning them. In this way your ad might attract special-interest buyers who wouldn't come to your sale otherwise. Items in this category might include big pieces of furniture, major appliances, tires, office equipment, hobby and sporting equipment, and true antiques.

Of course another factor in determining the size of your ad will be the amount of merchandise you have to sell. If you have just a few things to sell and they are of no great value, get the smallest ad you can. But if yours is a multifamily sale with a huge selection of merchandise, it would pay to run an extra-large ad, since the cost will be split among all participants.

There's no doubt that the bigger your ad, the more buyers you'll attract. It's just a matter of deciding at what point the higher ad costs will outweigh the additional revenue a bigger ad would bring.

If your sale's location is off the beaten path or would be difficult for strangers to find, your ads should include a landmark pinpointing the location or perhaps brief directions on how to get there.

Some sellers list their phone numbers along with their addresses, but I'd strongly advise against that. When the sale starts, you'll be busy enough taking money, wrapping merchandise, negotiating, answering questions, and otherwise "minding the store." A constantly ringing phone will be a serious distraction.

Another good argument against including your phone number is that many callers will inquire only about a specific item. If it has been sold or if for some reason they decide they don't want the item, they won't come to your sale. But if they don't have your phone number and must go to your sale to learn more about the item, they might see something else that interests them and buy that.

There are also sellers who put *nothing but* their phone numbers in their ads, omitting the address entirely. Yes, it's true that in this way you can screen callers to potential buyers who seem acceptable to you. But you'll also screen out most of your potential market. Many people are too timid to phone and others just won't bother.

OUTDOOR ADVERTISING

On the day of your sale you should have a big sign in front of your property where it can be seen easily by passing motorists.

If you live on a quiet side street, the sign needn't be large. But if you live on a street where motorists may be driving at a fast pace, it should be big enough to be read easily at a distance. Otherwise, drivers may miss it completely or may see it so late that they don't have time in which to stop safely.

One reason for the outside sign is to help people who have heard about your sale through newspaper or other advertising find your house or apartment. It's part of your overall strategy of making it as easy as possible for people to buy.

But another reason is that the sign itself will draw customers.

SIGNS ATTRACT PEOPLE

The degree to which outdoor signs alone will lure buyers is not fully appreciated by many people holding a sale for the first time.

Never underestimate the pulling power of a well-placed sign proclaiming "GARAGE SALE," "ESTATE SALE," "BASEMENT SALE," "PORCH SALE," or even the simple, magic word "SALE."

Every bargain-hunter, collector or junque addict who drives by and has a moment to spare will stop to see what you have to offer. It's a compulsion they can't help.

In fact the longer your sale goes on, the more important your signs become. After two days of a three-day sale, most of the people who have seen your newspaper or bulletin-board ads will have been there. A larger and larger proportion of your buyers will be casual passersby attracted solely by your sign.

HELP BUYERS FIND YOU

If your house or apartment is on a secluded side street or on a road with little traffic, you should also place signs on one or more busy arterial streets or highways near the site.

These signs should announce the sale, give the address, and perhaps include an arrow indicating the direction in which motorists should go. Good locations for such signs are at major intersections, where drivers slowing for a stop sign or traffic light will have time to see and read them.

Some sellers go to elaborate lengths with their outdoor advertising. They construct huge, sandwich-board signs for the front of their houses or decorate the site with ribbons and balloons, just as builders do when displaying model homes.

This is sound merchandising and imparts a touch of the carnival atmosphere which buyers seem to enjoy. But if you don't have the time or inclination for these ornate touches, don't worry. Any easy-to-read outdoor sign announcing your sale will do the job.

When making outdoor signs of any type, if there is any possibility of rain, use indelible markers. Otherwise, a shower may wash your signs out or make them so faint as to be unreadable. (But in marking your merchandise, do NOT use indelible markers. See Chapter 8.)

All About Pricing

Your most important preparation will be to put price tags on everything you hope to sell.

This can't be stressed too much. Yes, it takes time to price and tag everything, but you have much to lose and nothing to gain by not doing so.

Some sellers fail to price and tag their merchandise because they're lazy. Others intend to make price tags but don't allow enough time. Still others don't tag their things because of an odd notion that they may get higher prices by forcing buyers to make the first offer.

Nonsense. For each "better" deal you may get that way, you'll lose dozens of sales you could have made if your prices were marked.

WHY EVERYTHING SHOULD BE PRICED

The reasons for pricing everything are:

1. *To make it easier for people to buy.* All your preparations should be aimed at making it as easy as possible to buy. You can't expect people to seek you out to ask "how much is this" each time they see an item that interests them.

Look at it this way. How much time would *you* spend browsing through a variety store—and your sale is in effect a "variety store" of used goods—if you had to ask a clerk the price of everything on display (assuming the clerk wasn't too busy to talk to you because she was quoting prices to someone else)? Unless you had a very compelling interest in the item, you'd walk out and go to a store where prices are marked. And so will most of the people who come to your sale.

2. *To indentify bargains.* Many people who visit house and garage sales regularly have nothing specific in mind. They're there simply in hopes of finding bargains generally and will buy practically anything if they think the price is right. The only way to let them know that an item they didn't dream they wanted is a bargain is to put a price tag on it.

54

3. *To encourage buyers.* Many people are timid about asking prices. They don't want to get involved in haggling. But if they don't see a price on an item, they'll assume that the only way they can buy it is by haggling with you. Other people may assume that the absence of price tags means you're trying to put something over on them.

4. *To protect yourself.* Nobody can remember everything, especially if it's your first sale and you are confused by a lot of things suddenly happening at once. If you must quote prices off the top of your head, you'll risk making mistakes. If you quote too high a price, you'll kill the sale; and if your price is too low, you won't get as much as you should.

5. *To make the sale go smoothly.* If you've tagged all your merchandise, you won't have to spend all your time answering questions about how much this-or-that costs. You can concentrate on such more positive aspects of selling as pleasantly greeting arrivals, stressing an item's strong points, and completing sales.

HOW MUCH SHOULD IT COST?

In a book of this kind, it would be impossible to give meaningful advice on exact prices to charge for specific items of merchandise at a house or garage sale.

To begin with, an almost infinite variety of merchandise is offered at these sales, ranging from used clothing and the most commonplace household artifacts to the entire spectrum of "collectibles" and antiques. To be even partially comprehensive, any such pricing guide would have to take up hundreds or thousands of pages.

Also, any used item's value is affected by its condition. People in the trade sometimes observe that "you can't put a price on an antique." This is also true of used household goods. It means each item is unique. Over the years, it has acquired its own nicks, dents, scratches, scars, or other signs of wear and is now unlike any other item anywhere.

Further, there are regional variations in price levels. For instance, generally speaking, antique prices are lower on the East Coast than in the West. Most antiques come from the East because in the nineteenth century, the West was sparsely populated.

In addition, there may be fluctuations in prices for seasonal and other reasons. If you live where snow falls in winter, you will get a better price for used snow tires in December than in May. And when collectors decide to begin accumulating heretofore ignored items, as they did recently with so-called "Depression glass" dishes mass marketed in the 1930's, prices can rise rapidly. (Note: prices can also fall rapidly when, for one reason or another, items fall out of favor with collectors.)

Again, this is why it is such a good idea to visit other garage sales, rummage sales, flea markets, resale shops and antique shops and shows before holding your own sale. Knowing what you have to sell, you can note the range in which other people are attempting to sell these items. The closer you can price your merchandise to the lower end of this range, the easier it will be to sell it.

YOU CAN'T ASK STORE PRICES IN A GARAGE

Many first-time sellers underprice their merchandise. Usually this is because they are ignorant of the value of much of what they are selling. This is especially the case with elderly people who don't realize that some of the "everyday" things accumulated in their younger years are now desired by collectors.

But a more common mistake made by inexperienced sellers is to set prices too high.

There's a familiar saying to the effect that "a little knowledge is a dangerous thing." For many people, this is all too true when they get around to setting prices at their garage sale.

They've seen a certain item priced at X-dollars at a store or antique shop; they assume that a like item which they are selling is "worth" that too.

But it isn't. The main thing to remember is that when establishing prices for a house or garage sale, you are not competing with retail stores and antique shops, you are competing with people running other house and garage sales.

To put it another way: People will not pay retail prices for things they buy from strangers in basements and garages.

YOU'RE IN A "WHOLESALE MARKET"

When you buy from a store, the store's name and reputation stand behind the purchase. Be it a seller of new merchandise or an antique shop, the store usually offers some or all of the following: return privileges, check-cashing privileges, the extension of credit, a guarantee or warranty, and many other special services.

This means that to be truly competitive, your prices must be substantially below store prices. As we've noted earlier, house and garage sales are part of a wholesale market that supplies retail antique and junque shops. Indeed, although they may not identify themselves, some of your customers will be the owners of antique and resale shops.

It's true you can violate pricing rules and make some sales at high prices to *uninformed* buyers, but your total sales volume will be less than if you priced your merchandise realistically. Don't kid yourself. The people who go to these sales include some of the shrewdest shoppers in your town. That's why they're poking around in your garage instead of browsing in stores.

Of course there are special circumstances under which you may be able to buy items at retail, and turn around and sell them at your garage or house sale at a profit. These include items bought at genuine discount or "going out of business" sales. They also include things acquired in other sections of the country, where price levels may be lower or where you can obtain merchandise not available locally.

YOU CAN'T WIN THEM ALL

Pricing for a house or garage sale is at best an inexact science. Your general pricing strategy will depend on your reason for holding the sale. If it's to clean out your attic or to dispose of as much stuff as possible before moving, you'll price lower than if you hope to "get your money back" or show a profit.

In any event, when setting prices you're bound to make mistakes. You can't know the value of everything. You'll price some items too high and others too low, so after devoting a reasonable amount of time to your market research, don't spend too much time trying to determine the "best" price for every item. Antique and resale shop dealers make pricing mistakes too. Just go through what you have and set prices you think are reasonable.

When your sale starts, you can suspect that many of the items eagerly snatched up in the first hour were probably priced too low. And when it ends, you can conclude that much of the merchandise still unsold was priced too high.

Here are two good general pricing rules:

1. Try to set prices at less than people would pay for an item at a store, but more than you'd get for it if you sold it to a dealer.

2. Try to set the highest price at which people can't resist buying the item even if they don't need it.

TO BARGAIN OR NOT TO BARGAIN?

Some people who come to your sale will offer to buy items for less than the prices on your tags. Haggling is part of the game to them. No matter how low your price is to begin with, they'll always try to get it for less.

How you handle them depends on a lot of things, including your ability and willingness to engage in bargaining sessions.

If you'd rather not haggle, then set a "firm price" policy and stick to it. If your prices are reasonable, it's not a bad policy, either. Most people who make offers won't be offended if you turn them down in a courteous way. If your price is fair and they want the item, they'll probably buy anyhow.

Certainly the safest policy would be to set your tag prices at or not too far above your "rock bottom" price. Of course you'll have more pricing leeway on some items than on others. You should decide before the sale starts how far you'll be willing to lower your prices in a bargaining session.

If you want to be a real gambler, you can price all your merchandise substantially over what you regard as your "rock bottom" and then be prepared to haggle over everything. But to do this you must also be a thick-skinned extrovert. This tactic will also cut you off from buyers who don't want to haggle and risks alienating people who will decide you are a price gouger.

KEEP AN OPEN MIND

Even if you don't want to bargain, the prices on your tags should not be totally inflexible. Circumstances under which you should be willing to lower prices during your sale include:

•   If you learn that what you honestly thought was a fair price is actually much too high. An informed buyer may point out the discrepancy and convincingly prove it to you, perhaps with a pricing guide.

- If, after the sale has been going on for a while, you decide it would be better to sell something far below your tag price rather than be stuck with it unsold.

- If someone offers to buy a large number of items from you and asks for a price concession on the basis of his volume purchase. Under those circumstances, the buyer is entitled to a break. He is absorbing in one transaction some items which very possibly you would not otherwise sell.

It would be wise to avoid any such "volume purchase" discounts in the early hours of your sale. But the longer your sale goes on, the better those deals will be for you.

Last-Minute Preparations

8

Much of your time in the day or so before the sale will be spent setting prices, tagging merchandise, and then arranging your merchandise displays.

The more merchandise you have, the more time you should allow. The job should be virtually completed before your sale starts.

WHAT KIND OF TAGS?

A lot of people, some dealers included, use ordinary masking tape to make their "price tags." This is the cheapest tagging system. You cut off a piece of tape, affix it to the item, and mark the price.

But if you use masking tape, be aware of these drawbacks. It's the slowest method. If you have several hundred items to tag, it takes a lot of extra time to pull tape off the roll and hand-cut each "tag" with scissors. What's more, not all writing instruments mark effectively on masking tape's rough, somewhat absorbent surface. It's also the sloppiest-looking way to tag merchandise, and if you're using an indelible marker, there are circumstances under which the item could be damaged. The marker fluid can penetrate masking tape and adhere permanently to some surfaces. The glue on the tape itself is also more likely to cause damage than is true with most other types of tags.

By all means, do NOT use conventional gummed mailing labels. They are very difficult to remove and can permanently damage some surfaces.

With some types of marking instruments, prices can be marked directly onto glass, metal, porcelain, pottery, and other hard, washable surfaces. But if you do this, *be sure you are not using an indelible marker. The marks must be easy to wipe or wash off.*

Never put ANY mark directly on merchandise until you've experimented and are SURE the marks can be removed. To be on the safe side, don't mark any item directly unless it's a low-priced item.

One satisfactory way to mark items is with paper fastened by transparent tape. While cumbersome, this system is inexpensive and relatively safe.

If you're willing to spend a dollar or two, invest in a box of self-applicating, adhesive tags, available in larger stationery and office-supply stores. The more items you must tag, the more this investment will pay for itself in time and convenience.

Tags of this type are easy to apply and relatively easy to remove. Your customers will appreciate that and so will you. As your sale progresses, you may decide to change some prices. Switching tags is easier and quicker with these tags than with any other marking system. And when the sale is over, it'll be easy to remove these tags from your unsold merchandise.

No matter what system you use, be careful. Don't put tags or marks where they can't be removed easily without risking damage to the item.

CLEAN UP YOUR MERCHANDISE

One thing which people who have held successful sales stress almost uniformly is the importance of making your merchandise as attractive and serviceable as you reasonably can.

Items that are clean and in good shape will get higher prices than like items covered with dust or in disrepair.

Don't knock yourself out trying to polish every rusty old garden implement. But dishes, glassware, and crockery should be washed, clothing and linens should be cleaned, furniture and pictures should be dusted, and silver should be polished.

You should also make any simple, obvious repairs. It wouldn't pay to get bogged down in major fix-up jobs, but it only takes a minute or so to drive a nail or apply a dab of paint or glue.

POINT-OF-SALE SIGNS

Your last-minute preparations will include making your outside "GARAGE SALE" signs, as well as other signs to be posted in the streets. This subject is covered in Chapter 6, "How To Advertise Your Sale."

But you may also need some point-of-sale signs. For instance, if your merchandise is to be displayed in two or more locations, signs should announce that fact. You may put some merchandise outside in your yard or patio, with the remainder in a basement or on a back porch. A sign in the yard should clearly indicate that there is more to see, and an arrow should point the way.

If your sale is in your basement, porch, or some other part of your home, put up a sign indicating the door through which you want people to enter. If it's not necessary for people to ring or knock, put a "PLEASE WALK IN" sign on the door. (And when your sale ends, don't forget to take THAT sign down immediately.)

Other types of signs you may want in your sale area include:

- Information about merchandise not displayed in the sale area. Some pieces of furniture may be too heavy to move there.

Other items may be so fragile or valuable that you don't want them handled casually by curiosity-seekers.

• More information about items you're selling. If a piece is especially old or has some novel or unique aspects, a small sign should point that out.

• "NOT FOR SALE" signs on anything in the sale area you don't want to sell and would rather not have examined, handled, and possibly damaged.

BE READY TO MAKE CHANGE

Making change will become less and less of a problem after your sale runs for a while. But if you're not able to make change during the opening hours, you could inconvenience your customers. This could even cost you a sale or two and in any event would distract you from more important business.

If you anticipate a fair volume of business, be ready with a fair supply of nickles and dimes saved from your pocket change during the weeks before the sale. Then, a day or so before your sale, go to a bank and get a roll of quarters (ten dollars' worth), twenty one-dollar bills, a few five-dollar bills, and at least one ten-dollar bill.

KNOW WHAT YOU'LL DO WITH YOUR MONEY

You'll also need a plan for handling your money. It's not likely anyone will come to your sale with the idea of stealing it, but there's no point being so careless that you'll risk being victimized.

Most of the cash you accumulate during a sale will be in the form of currency. It will be safer on your person than in a cigar box, purse, or other container that may, for one reason or another, be left unattended, no matter how briefly.

One idea would be to keep your currency in a money clip. A man can store the clip in his trousers pocket; a woman can keep it in a deep pocket in a dress, sweater, or coat. Either way, the clip is easy to reach. At the same time, you won't have to expose a bulky wallet that may also contain valuable papers, credit cards, etc.

If you're doing a brisk sales volume, currency may stack up quickly. Periodically, it would be prudent to take out some bills and secrete them in a secure part of your house or apartment rather than display too big a pile in front of strangers.

You'll also accumulate a lot of silver. Coins are too heavy to store in a pocket. Instead, put them in a box or other container. Then establish a system for keeping the box under observation and control at all times.

HAVE A CREDIT POLICY

Anyone selling merchandise to the public should have a policy on extending credit. The house and garage sale is no exception.

If you have a fair number of items priced at several dollars and more, sooner or later someone will probably ask if you'll take a personal check in payment.

If you think you'd feel uncomfortable at the idea of taking a check instead of cash, plan ahead what you'll say and how you'll say it, so you won't offend a customer with a hasty, unintentionally rude remark.

The best thing would be to explain as cordially as you can that there's nothing personal in your decision, but you're simply not prepared to handle checks; that you're terribly sorry, but yours is strictly a cash-and-carry sale.

If you have firmly decided on this policy in advance, it would be a good idea to place a sign prominently in your sales area stating "ALL SALES CASH, PLEASE," or "NO CHECKS, PLEASE."

There is always some risk in accepting checks from strangers. On the other hand, if you don't accept checks, you might miss some big sales. Many people simply don't carry much cash with them. They always pay for things with checks or credit cards, and may be offended no matter how politely you turn them down.

One way of handling the would-be buyer who doesn't have enough cash is to accept a deposit, and then to hold the item until the buyer returns with the full payment.

SET UP YOUR "COMMAND HEADQUARTERS"

In arranging your sale area, make a place for yourself. It should have a table or other flat working space, plus chairs for you and anyone helping you.

The location of your "command headquarters" will depend on your layout. All things being equal, it would be best to put it where you can greet people as they arrive and check them out as they leave.

Your headquarters should be equipped with:

- Marking and tagging equipment, for replacing lost or damaged tags or making tags with new prices.
- Sign-making equipment, for making signs the need for which may not be apparent until the sale gets underway. For instance, so many people may wander into nonsale areas that you'll decide you want some "PLEASE KEEP OUT" signs.
- Pencil and paper, for making computations when people buy more than one item. In this regard, if you own or can borrow a small adding machine, by all means use it. It'll save time and reduce errors.
- Record-keeping equipment, for logging sales of consigned items or crediting items sold at joint sales.

HELP THEM CARRY IT AWAY

In line with your policy of making it easy for people to buy, provide bags to help them carry the merchandise away.

During the month or so before the sale, put aside all paper bags you accumulate during your shopping trips. Haul them out on the day of your sale and store them at your command headquarters.

Your wrapping department should also include newspapers, for wrapping glassware and other fragile items; and some cardboard boxes for people who buy a lot of merchandise.

69

Don't Make It Look Too Much Like a Store

9

Your merchandise display should be attractive, but don't go overboard. Being neat and tidy is one thing. Dressing up your sales area to where it begins to resemble a store is something else.

At some so-called "garage" and "basement" sales, merchandise is professionally laid out in display cases and the atmosphere is that of a high-class (and high-priced) antique or gift shop.

70

This is a mistake. People go to garage and house sales in hopes of finding bargains sold by private parties. A too-professional atmosphere will intimidate some buyers.

In fact, if your sales area begins to look too much like a store, try hoking it up a bit with some "bargain boxes" and a general air of homey disarray.

DISPLAYING YOUR MERCHANDISE

Here are some tips on displaying your merchandise:

• Be sure all tables, benches, TV tables, and other objects holding merchandise are sturdy enough to remain standing even though jostled, which they almost inevitably will be.

• When laying out items on a counter or table, put the small items in front and the big ones in back. This will lessen the chances of items in front being knocked down when someone reaches out to inspect an item in the back.

• Pay special attention to the aisles. Is there enough room for people to move without bumping into one another and/or into your display tables? And are the aisles clear? One of the commonest errors first-time sellers make is to place lamps or other electrical appliances with the cords in or dangerously near an aisle. After your first customer stumbles over an electric cord, perhaps taking a lamp and/or display table down with her, you won't make that mistake again.

• If you are selling lamps or small electric appliances, have an outlet available where customers can test them.

- If at all possible, hang coats, dresses, jackets, sweaters, etc., on some kind of rack rather than pile them in a heap on a table. Buyers can see the clothing easier and it will take a lot less of a beating from people pawing over it. Also, if you are selling hats, outerwear, or other clothing which people might try on, have a mirror available.

- If you have a "quarter box," "penny box," or other box filled with merchandise jumbled together, be sure all the merchandise is sturdy and relatively impervious to damage. Things in those boxes sometimes take a terrific beating.

- It's all right to set merchandise on the floor or the ground under your tables, but don't block your tables. If there is any doubt, go out in the aisle yourself and play the role of a customer to be sure it will be easy for people to reach all the merchandise.

- If you are selling many pictures, hang them and/or spread them out by leaning them against a wall, fence, furniture, etc., rather than pile them into a box. Many people buy pictures on impulse. They don't even know they want a picture until they see the right one. Also, if you leave pictures piled in a box, they will be damaged by people rummaging through the box.

- Check the lighting in your sales area. On overcast days, the interiors of some garages and basements are dim and gloomy. If your sales area lacks adequate lighting, try rigging up some temporary extra lights so buyers can see what you have to sell. What they can't see, they won't buy.

- If you don't want an item handled, don't put it where it can BE handled. Store it on a high shelf or in a locked cabinet where only you can get it.

72

SPECIAL OUTDOOR PROBLEMS

If your display space is outdoors, you may face some special problems stemming from weather conditions.

Even a moderate gust of wind may knock tall, fragile items down. If it is a windy day and you have any items of this type displayed outside, it would be prudent to lay them on their sides rather than stand them up.

Another outdoor hazard is rain (or in the winter months, snow). If there is the merest threat of rain, have a contingency plan. Depending on the type of display and where it is, be ready either to move your merchandise inside or cover it. People who sell regularly at flea markets usually carry large plastic drop-cloths with them for this purpose.

Still another hazard is the sun. It can melt candles and even some glues if repairs have been made recently. If you'll be outdoors most of the time, it could also pose a hazard to you. Engrossed in the details of running your sale, you could suffer a painful case of sunburn. If you're not accustomed to being exposed to the sun for long periods, wear a broad-brimmed hat and something that covers your arms, no matter how warm the day.

SALES PROMOTION DEVICES

Depending on how much you have to sell, where you'll be holding your sale, and how much help you'll have, you may also wish to use one or more of these sales promotion devices:

- *A box of free items.* Obviously, the items you put in this box would be things of minimal value, but this is a psychologically effective device. It suggests that your main reason for holding the sale is to clean out your attic or closets, not to make a profit. Also, people taking items from a "free box" usually feel obliged to buy something, too. Of course, it won't pay to set up a free box if you don't have many items to sell. In that case, you'd be better off trying to get some money, no matter how small the sum, for all of your merchandise.
- *Free coffee or other refreshments.* This is especially effective on raw days. In addition to being a convenience your customers will appreciate, it will induce them to remain in the sales area for a longer period of time. This is good for two reasons. First, the longer they hang around, the more likely they will see something they want and buy it. Second, the longer they linger, the bigger the crowd; and the more people congregate, the more they will fall into the buying spirit.

Of course, you'll need a spacious sales area before considering whether or not to offer coffee or other refreshments. Also, you'll want to be sure you have enough people helping with your sale. You don't want to be wasting your time boiling water when customers are waiting with money in their hands.
- *Background music.* Just as in retail stores, a low-playing radio or hi-fi tends to put buyers at ease, especially during slack periods when few other buyers are present. It also gives them a sense of privacy in carrying out conversations among themselves not possible when "it's so quiet you can hear a pin drop."

Here Come the "Early Birds" 10

The more populous the area in which you live, the more likely that your last-minute preparations will be interrupted by visits from one or more "early birds."

These people aren't content merely to show up early on the day of the sale, a phenomenon you should accept with good humor.

No, the "early birds" want more. Usually they've learned of your sale through newspaper ads. On occasion they'll show up even before your ad appears, having heard of your sale through word-of-mouth. They'll have all manner of explanations as to why they're there so far in advance, although usually they'll appear the afternoon or evening of the day before your sale is to begin.

WHAT THESE PEOPLE REALLY WANT

Some will tell you they "won't have the car tomorrow, and can't I please see what you have tonight?" Others will say they're "going out of town," or "just happened to be in the neighborhood."

The variety of their cover stories is infinite. To make it more convincing, they might claim to be especially interested in a particular type of item, such as "a bookcase for my son, who is a student." But even if you say you have no bookcase, you'll be pressured into showing what you do have. And if you stammer something about how the sale isn't supposed to start until the following day, they'll say very convincingly: "But you want to *sell* your things, don't you? What difference does it make when you sell them?"

Whatever they say, you must recognize these "early birds" for what they are. Nearly all are semiprofessional dealers or hard-core junque addicts. They're trying to take advantage of your confusion and inexperience to buy something valuable for as close to nothing as possible.

They're hoping your merchandise will include treasures whose true value you fail to recognize. They want to snatch up those bargains before anyone else does. Many also know that in the confusing hours before the sale, you haven't had time to establish all your prices. You may be rattled by their approach and inadvertently quote too low a price off the top of your head, or accept a ridiculously low offer.

SHOULD YOU—OR SHOULDN'T YOU?

All that being the case, should you allow these "early birds" into your house, garage, or what have you one or more days before the sale, or shouldn't you?

Many people buy the argument that since they want to sell all of their possessions anyway, it doesn't matter if they sell some ahead of time.

If you're in that camp—and based on interviews with people who have held sales, you have plenty of company—just be on guard. You could take a real beating by allowing an "early bird" to prowl through your things before all your prices are set, offering a dollar for this or a quarter for that or wondering "if you couldn't reduce the price a little, it seems so high. . . ."

Other people stoutly refuse to allow "early birds" into their homes or apartments until the day of the sale. Certainly you should have no conscience qualms about politely but firmly telling an "early bird" that you're not ready yet, and haven't the time.

WHY WE DON'T LET THEM IN

Unless they are your friends or neighbors, I'd recommend against allowing any "early birds" into your house or apartment until the day of the sale because:

- It isn't fair to customers who do abide by the rules.
- It's more important for you to complete your last-minute preparations—pricing, making signs, cleaning merchandise, setting up your display area, etc.—than it is to drop everything to show one "early bird" around.
- Anything the "early birds" might buy before a sale starts, they will also buy *after* it starts. If you won't let them in the day before the sale, almost invariably they'll be first in line in the morning.
- Unless you have badly underpriced your merchandise, "early birds" don't buy much anyhow. If an "early bird" begins buying right and left, your things were worth a lot more than you thought.
- Many "early birds" are doing what they do because they want to take advantage of you. Why encourage them?
- Finally, all "early birds" are guilty of calculated rudeness. When you place an ad announcing your sale, you are inviting buyers to your house on the sale dates, and no other. If you were invited to a friend's house for dinner on Sunday, you wouldn't show up on Saturday to announce: "I'm sorry, but I'm hungry now, so feed me today instead." Yet this is precisely what the "early birds" are doing to you.

For what it's worth, professionals who make a business of holding house, estate, and garage sales for a fee refuse to allow any "early birds" inside ahead of time. In addition to being unfair to their other buyers, they know from experience that anything an "early bird" buys would be snatched up in the sale's opening hours anyhow.

Security at Your Sale

Hopefully, you won't have any security problems at your sale. The vast majority of people interviewed in the preparation of this book reported no security problems whatsoever.

However, it would be prudent to anticipate any security problems that might arise and to take what precautions you can to hold risks to a minimum.

The two aspects of security are potential crimes against your property and potential crimes against your person.

One of the best defenses against both is to have as many people helping with your sale as you can. If possible, at least two people should be present at all times.

GUARDING AGAINST SHOPLIFTERS

Anyone who sells merchandise to the public risks being victimized by shoplifters. No neighborhoods are immune to them.

In fact, shoplifting problems in wealthy suburbs are often as serious as anywhere else. Well-to-do housewives and children from affluent families may steal for psychological reasons that have nothing to do with the value of the merchandise.

It's not likely you would be visited by professional shoplifters. Those people confine their efforts to stealing fast-moving new merchandise at stores. Another thing in your favor is that some people who might steal from stores, rationalizing that the store can afford the loss, might not be willing to steal from a private party.

But you could be visited by some amateur shoplifters, and the first rule in guarding against them is to be reasonably alert at all times. This doesn't require following people around and watching their every move. However, try to be aware of what's going on. Some shoplifters try to strike during a sale's first hours, when sellers are busiest. Especially watch customers who dawdle for long periods in far-off corners for no apparent reason.

Another rule is *to watch people who watch you.* Most amateur shoplifters are self-conscious. Before pocketing an item, they will keep glancing at the owner of the merchandise to see if they are being observed.

Other precautions include:

- If you display merchandise in more than one room, try to have someone helping with the sale posted in every room. If this is not possible, concentrate the easy-to-steal items in rooms that will be watched and put larger, bulkier pieces in other rooms.
- If you're selling items of considerable value, display them under lock-and-key, perhaps in a locked cabinet.
- If you're selling small, easy-to-conceal items, such as jewelry, put them in or near your "command headquarters," so it will be easy for you to watch the display.

DON'T LEAVE YOUR "STORE" UNATTENDED

Certainly any time you leave your "store" unattended, you invite the possibility of theft. At least one person should be in the sales area whenever customers are present.

A common tactic used by shoplifters working in pairs or groups is for one to distract the seller while the others steal what they can. Any seller alone in the sales area should be alert to this possibility.

Another tactic is to attempt to lure the seller away from the sales area. In the case of garage sales, often this is done by sending someone to buy one or more bulky items. This person then asks for help in carrying these items to a car.

While the sellers are so engaged, the "buyer's" confederates, perhaps hidden down the alley, will hurry into the garage and steal as much as they can carry, probably heading first for the seller's cashbox.

HOW TO HANDLE SHOPLIFTERS

If a shoplifter victimizes you, it's not likely you'll catch him in the act. You probably won't notice until the thief has left or until the sale is over that an item is missing.

Then you may think back and recall that the last time you saw the item, it was being handled by a customer. In many cases you'll be certain in your own mind who stole the item, although you'll have no way of proving it.

The best way to handle people whose actions have made you suspicious would be to begin devoting an inordinate amount of attention to them. *Follow them wherever they go; keep asking them what they're interested in buying, and if you can help them in any way.* If they have larceny on their mind, they'll soon get discouraged and leave.

But you must be on very solid ground before actually accusing anyone of shoplifting. Merely being "sure" someone stole an item isn't enough. Unless you or someone helping you with the sale actually saw the item being taken, it's always possible you made a mistake.

The laws of arrest are complex and vary from state to state. Law-enforcement officers themselves often have a difficult time interpreting them correctly.

Certainly as a private citizen you should never even consider attempting to physically detain a shoplifter unless the item you wish to recover is of very great value to you. Aside from the fact that you could be injured if the shoplifter resisted, you could lay yourself open to criminal and civil charges if the courts found that you used unreasonable force in trying to detain someone. Just ask yourself: Is it really worth the recovery of the item to assume those legal and physical risks?

To be on the safe side, no matter what happens, *never touch a shoplifter.* If you see an item stolen, tell the suspect what you have seen and ask for the return of the item. If the shoplifter refuses, announce that you will call the police and ask the suspect to remain until the police arrive. If the shoplifter leaves before the police get there, get the license number of the suspect's car.

Again, most people interviewed in the preparation of this book reported no shoplifting problems. But if you encounter any, weigh the value of what was taken against the problems you could create by making a false accusation or getting involved in a physical altercation with the suspect.

OTHER SECURITY PROBLEMS

If you live in a neighborhood where crimes of violence are a constant threat, you probably wouldn't consider holding a house or apartment sale under any circumstances.

But no matter where you live, any time you open your residence or any part of it to strangers visiting your sale, you create potential hazards to yourself and to your property.

84

The most serious possibility is that of a crime against your person. This is not likely when several customers are present, but when you are alone with a single customer it is always at least conceivable.

This reemphasizes why it's a good idea to have at least one other person helping you with your sale, especially if you are a woman or a senior citizen living alone. In any event, when alone with a customer capable of intimidating you physically, be especially alert.

Another potential hazard is that of burglary after the sale is over, inspired by something a would-be burglar or his accomplice may have seen when visiting your sale.

To reduce this possibility, give customers as little opportunity as possible to learn that you own anything worth breaking in to steal. Don't allow strangers into any part of your home where they can observe valuables that are not for sale.

Especially, don't try to sell anything that would suggest that you are a serious collector of such small, easy-to-carry valuables as fine jewelry, stamps, or coins.

If you want to sell fine jewelry, stamps, coins, or other items of great value, do so through an established dealer or through an auction rather than attempt to sell them to strangers who come to your house or apartment.

Similarly, unless you live in a rural area where the ownership and use of firearms is commonplace, it would be prudent not to try to sell firearms of any age or condition at your house or garage sale, or to in any way let it be known to your customers that you own or collect firearms.

The Sale Begins— and You're on Your Own

12

As you can see by now, the real secret to running a successful house or garage sale lies in the effort you're willing to put into getting ready for it. The more thorough the preparations, the more successful your sale will be and the easier it will go.

No matter how hard you try, you probably won't be completely ready when people begin showing up on the first day. The first arrivals will be there earlier than the time you advertised, and before you know it, the sale will be on full-swing.

But if you've followed the advice in this book, at least you'll be pretty far along. You'll also be ready for some of the problems that may arise.

Once buyers begin pawing through your things, you're on your own. Those first few hours will be your busiest. And after those first few hours, you'll also be pretty far along toward being an "old pro" at holding house and garage sales.

YOU AND YOUR CUSTOMERS

If you've never "met the public" before, your first sale will be an eye-opening experience.

All sorts of people will show up. Most will be courteous and considerate, but there may be exceptions.

Some people may be thoughtless, others may be careless, and still others may be overtly rude, perhaps commenting loudly on how items are priced too high or otherwise poor-mouthing what you have to sell. The most boorish of them may even criticize your house and/or your housekeeping.

Whatever they say, don't let it bother you. Consider it part of your education in the mysterious workings of human nature.

Although it hardly ever happens, it's also conceivable that a visitor at your sale may so overstep the bounds of propriety as to become abusive or belligerent. In this case, you have every right to politely ask the visitor to leave, and if the visitor refuses, to call the police.

Your own personality will go a long way toward determining how you'll handle your customers. Do what you feel most comfortable doing. If you've had sales experience, you don't need any advice from this book; if you haven't, don't worry. Just use common sense.

In general, don't be standoffish or aloof. Try to make people feel at home. If someone seems especially interested in an item, tell him a little about it. You can often clinch a sale that way.

On the other hand, don't force yourself on people. Don't dog their footsteps and volunteer a lot of information they aren't asking for, or start quoting below-tag prices on items they've picked up merely to examine casually.

To put it another way, treat people at your sale the way you'd want to be treated if you went to someone else's sale.

THEY WON'T ALL BUY

Accept cheerfully the fact that for one reason or another, many people who come to your sale won't buy anything. Make them feel at home anyhow.

Who knows? That person may be back later to buy, or may mention your sale to someone else who'll drop in and take your biggest white elephant off your hands. No matter how uninterested people seem to be, give them a friendly "thanks for coming" as they leave.

HONESTY REALLY IS THE BEST POLICY

Trying to hide flaws in the items you're trying to sell isn't just dishonest, it simply doesn't pay. The flaws will probably be detected anyway. By being honest with your customers you'll win their respect, not to mention your own self-respect. You'll also sell more than you would otherwise.

Some sellers who ordinarily are the most honest of citizens will lose their perspective when they hold a garage sale. They not only fail to point out serious flaws in their merchandise, they try to conceal them through such crude gambits as covering them with price tags.

All you can get with trickery of this kind is trouble. An angry buyer may return with an item later to demand his money back. No matter how graciously you handle that situation, your image will suffer. All potential buyers within earshot will walk off without buying anything, and they'll tell their friends and neighbors what they overheard.

All expensive glassware, porcelain, fine art, etc., that is chipped, cracked, or otherwise flawed should have an "AS IS" notation on its tag. If appliances or other mechanical devices don't work or need repairs, this should also be noted on the tag or told to potential buyers.

LEARN AS YOU GO ALONG

As your sale proceeds, be ready to make changes based on what you see and hear.

For instance, if there isn't enough room for people to move through your "aisles," clear a bigger space. If people are knocking items down or tripping over wires or other obstructions, get those things out of the traffic pattern.

If people are ignoring items because they're difficult to reach or see, put those items in a more accessible location. If a motorist drawn by your sign says he almost missed your sale because the sign is too small or is hidden behind a tree, make a bigger sign or get your sign out in the open.

If a lot of people show up in the first hour or two but hardly anyone buys anything, your prices are probably much too high. Be ready at any time to review prices and lower those you conclude you innocently set at too high a level.

Many sellers wait until the end of their sale to start lowering prices, but the longer you wait the less good this will do. Remember, the largest number of potential buyers will probably arrive at the beginning of your sale. If your sale spans several days, relatively few buyers will turn up in the final hours.

WHEN THE SALE IS OVER

When the sale is over, you'll be faced with the pleasant task of counting your money and the unpleasant one of putting back into storage all the things you didn't sell. If you took in a lot of money, it might be a good idea to deposit most of it in a bank as soon as possible.

One thing you should do right away is to take down your signs, especially your outdoor advertising signs.

First, this is to avoid inconveniencing people who might see the signs and drive to your sale not knowing it is over. Second, it will avoid inconveniencing you with unexpected and unwanted guests hours or days after the sale has ended. Finally, it is just good manners.

Occasionally, weather-beaten garage- or house-sale signs will remain posted on trees and telephone poles weeks after the sale, which is hardly a contribution to community beautification. What's more, if enough people did that, another result could be action by the city council or county board to place onerous restrictions on the placement of all house- and garage-sale signs.

If you think you might hold another sale, another thing you might do when your first sale is over is to sit down as soon as you can and write a critique. Sum up everything you've learned during the sale and note what you'd do differently next time while the details are still fresh in your mind.

Note also what you had observed about the effectiveness of your advertising. How did most people hear about your sale? Through your newspaper ads, your signs, word-of-mouth, or what? And note the price levels at which various categories of items seemed to sell best, as well as the types of items people seemed to want most and the types they ignored.

Then put your critique away until your next sale, when you can take it out and refresh your memory.

Whether you hold another sale or not, your first one will give you a fellowship with anyone else who has ever sold household goods, be it from a residence, a flea market, a resale shop, or through an auctioneer.

By displaying this initiative, you have responded to an ageless urge to get the most you reasonably can for whatever it is you have to offer, which is what makes the wheels of commerce turn.

APPENDIX A

HOUSE AND GARAGE SALE CHECKLIST

Before the Sale

Things to Decide

Where will you hold your sale?
When will you hold your sale?
Will you hold it alone or jointly?
Will you take consignments?
Will you bargain for prices or hold firm?
How will you handle your money during the sale?
Will you accept checks or insist on all cash?
What kind of "price tags" will you use?
Where will you put your "command headquarters?"
Will you offer free coffee or other refreshments?
If any "early birds" show up while you are preparing for your sale, will you let
    them in?

Things to Do

Market research:
- Visit other garage and house sales to check price levels and learn from other sellers.
- Visit resale shops, antique shops, and shows, etc., to see if any of your things are "collectible."

Place newspaper advertisements.
Place sale notices on bulletin boards, in store windows, etc.
Clean up merchandise; make minor repairs.
Make signs for:
- Outdoor advertising.
- Point-of-sale information.

Get money for change before sale starts.
Price and tag merchandise.
Display merchandise.
Set up "command headquarters" equipped with:
- Changebox.
- Bags and newspapers, for wrapping.
- Sign-making equipment, including signboard or white paper, scissors, markers, and transparent tape for affixing signs.

After the Sale

Take down outdoor signs.
Take down advertising cards on bulletin boards, in store windows, etc.
Take cash to financial institution.
Write a post mortem if you plan to hold another sale.

APPENDIX B

KEEPING RECORDS FOR JOINT AND CONSIGNMENT SALES

If you must keep records of joint or consignment sales, any system that works and is fully understood by all parties concerned will do, no matter how simple or complicated.

The following three systems are suggested only as a starting point. Any number of variations stemming from them are possible.

The first two of the following examples have the advantage of great simplicity.

The third, for consignment sales only, is suggested primarily because it provides a complete list of consigned items. If the items are of some value, this would be a protection for both your consignors and you.

This is one of the simplest ways to keep records for a joint sale or consignment sellers.

Merely rule off a column for each seller. Sellers tag their own items, identifying each tag with an initial or code number.

Then list the items as each sale is made, either by price alone or by price and a description of the article, as is done below.

HELEN (CODE "H")	JOAN (CODE "J")	SUE (CODE "S")
FIGURINE- .25	CHAIR - 3.00	PICTURE- 7.00
PICTURE FRAME — .50	TABLE - 4.00	WOOD BOX- .50
	LAMP - 7.00	BICYCLE -15.00
DISH— .25	TYPEWRITER-15.00	OLD BOTTLE .25
SOFA — 6.00		MISC. CHILDS CLOTHES— .75

Another simple system is to have sellers or consignors tag their own items with coded, removable tags.

Then, as each item is sold, remove the tag and paste it to the "sold" sheet under the seller's or consignor's name, as is done below.

If you use this system, someone in the selling group must be given the responsibility of removing tags as each item is sold.

HELEN (CODE "H")	JOAN (CODE "J")	SUE (CODE "S")
H / 25¢	J / 3.00	S / 1.00
H / 50¢	J / 4.00	S / 50¢
H / 25¢	J / 1.00	S / 15.00
H / 75¢	J / 15.00	S / 25¢
H / 6.00		

If you want a record of all items brought to you by consignors, have them provide you with a list.

They must also tag their items, identifying tags with code numbers keyed to their lists. For instance, if a consignor's code letter is "H," the consignor lists and tags his items as "H-1," "H-2," etc., as in the example below.

Using this system, you can check out each item on the list when the lot is brought to you, to be sure all merchandise is actually received. Then you check items out as they are sold. If you wish, you could also make a notation on the list when you pay a consignor for a sold item.

The big advantage of this system is that it puts the burden of preparing the list and tagging the items entirely on the consignor. However, its effectiveness will depend on the consignor's ability to draw up a legible and workable list.

CONSIGNOR: HELEN (CODE LETTER "H")

ITEM NO.	DESCRIPTION	PRICE	SOLD	PAID HELEN
H-1	OIL LAMP	5.00	✓	
H-2	OAK CHAIR	8.00	✓	✓
H-3	SET OF DISHES	3.00		
H-4	BLUE GLASS VASE	4.00		
H-5	NEW ELECTRIC TOASTER	8.00		
H-6	OLD STERLING DISH	10.00	✓	

APPENDIX C

TYPICAL NEWSPAPER ADS

GARAGE & Yard Sale: Fri. Sat. Sun. Jul. 7-8-9, 9 to 6 p.m. Household treasures, furniture, and fine junk. 2550 East Evans, Spr.

BASEMENT Sale: July 8, 9. Coin Coll., $40, Instamatic, $5, tape recorder, $20, more. 120 Pine. Newton

BACKYARD sale—July 8. Many antiques. 211 E. Prospect. Spr.

GARAGE Sale. Fri., Sat. S-C typewriter, Victorian chair, tools, Maytag washer & dryer, misc. 1262 Mead

HOUSE Sale
813 Grant St., Spr.
Thurs. July 6—9:30-7:30
Fri. July 7—9:30-5:00
4 piece cherry living room set, hutch cupboard, 3 piece light oak bedroom set, desk lamps, mirror, mangle, refrigerator, electric dryer, wrought iron chandelier, assorted tables, set golf clubs, odds and ends.

APT. SALE, Sat. & Sun. July 8, 9, 9:30-6:30. 609 Ridge, Springfield. Bedroom suite, kitchen utensils,